The Nation's Favourite Prayers

Written by David Winter

Prayers compiled and introduced by Su Box

LION

A Lion Book
an imprint of
Lion Hudson plc
Mayfield House, 256 Banbury Road,
Oxford OX2 7DH, England
www.lionhudson.com
ISBN-13: 978-0-7459-5211-6
ISBN-10: 0-7459-5211-9

First edition 2006
10 9 8 7 6 5 4 3 2 1 0

Acknowledgments
pp. 58, 59: The Lord's Prayer and 'Hail Mary' taken from the
English translation of the Roman Missal © 1973, International
Committee on English in the Liturgy, Inc. All rights reserved.
pp. 69, 85, 86: 'Lord, bless this food', 'Almighty God, Father of
all mercies' and 'O God, the creator and preserver of all mankind'
taken from The Book of Common Prayer, the rights in which are
vested in the Crown, and reproduced by permission of the Crown's
Patentee, Cambridge University Press.
pp. 88, 90: 'Almighty God, to whom all hearts are open' and 'Father
of all' taken from The Book of Common Worship, published by
Church House Publishing, 2000.
p. 95: Extract taken from The Desert by Minnie Louise Haskins.

A catalogue record for this book is available
from the British Library

Typeset in 11/14 Berkeley Oldstyle BT
Printed and bound in Great Britain
by Cox & Wyman Ltd, Reading

The
Nation's Favourite
Prayers

Contents

Foreword

This book largely wrote itself. At its heart is a collection of the 'nation's favourite prayers', chosen simply because they *are* 'favourites': well used, well tuned and well loved by thousands and millions of people. In some cases they have been on the lips of British people for many centuries; a few are relatively modern. All could be described as the authentic voice of the nation at prayer.

And, somewhat to the surprise of everyone who tries to measure it, this nation *does* pray. Church-going, as a regular weekly activity, may have been on the decline for the past sixty or seventy years, but there is strong evidence (not least in this selection of their prayers) that British people have never given up on prayer. During the Second World War, by which time church-going was already in serious decline, the 'National Days of Prayer' evoked a staggering response. Churches and chapels were full to overflowing, with people standing in the doorways and aisles, to pray for peace – and, doubtless, victory over a cruel and malign foe.

In my own parish ministry, I made a practice of asking people I visited whether they would like me to say a prayer before leaving them. I never had a single person decline the offer, even those who had assured me that they were 'not believers'. There seems to be something in the very nature of humanity that longs to pray, to establish contact with a beneficent power beyond and far greater than ourselves with whom (or with which) we may share our concerns, problems and needs.

So the collection of 'favourite prayers' is the heart of this book. Preceding it, there are eight short chapters on the subject of prayer, looking at what it is; why people feel the urge to pray; how and when prayer can best be said; and how a 'beginner' might go about doing it. There is also a longer chapter on the most frequently expressed problems and difficulties relating to prayer.

Prayer is certainly *not* the preserve of the 'professional' – the priest, minister or monk. Far from it. At its heart it is the most democratic practice imaginable – open to all, free of charge and with unlimited access to the very utmost source of power. It would seem to be folly of the highest order not even to explore its significance and its possibilities, or to turn our backs on the wonderful spiritual heritage that these 'favourite prayers' provide for us.

David Winter

1

Prayer is Natural

'All we can do is pray'

> **'**The wish to pray is
> a prayer in itself.**'**
>
> Georges Bernanos,
> *Diary of a Country Priest*

The distraught relative stands in front of the camera, fighting back the tears. 'All we can do is pray,' she says, and every viewer the world over knows what she means. The situation is hopeless; we feel helpless, stranded and alone. We can do nothing ourselves – we can't effect the hostage's release; we can't heal the terminal cancer; we can't get in touch with the loved one who has disappeared in an earthquake. 'All we can do is pray.' In those circumstances, there's nothing abnormal or odd about praying. It's what most of us would do.

When the search began for 'the nation's favourite prayers', it would have seemed odd to start with the ones that are uttered most often, or with the deepest feeling: 'Oh God, no!' (when we hear of someone's death), 'God help us' (when the pension scheme goes bust), and more positively, 'Thank God' (when we hear that the child is safe after all). God is in fact endlessly invoked in our everyday speech, sometimes carelessly or casually ('Oh my God!'), and sometimes with blasphemous or at least imprecatory intent. As the second New York tower was struck by a plane on 11 September 2001, with a terrifying explosion and fireball, a watcher down on the street was caught on an idle radio microphone. He uttered just two words, in what can only be described as awestruck tones: 'Jesus Christ'. I doubt if that was either imprecatory or blasphemous. What other name, what other recourse to understanding could one have than the name and title of the world's saviour?

So in one sense prayer is natural. It is not difficult to introduce even very young children to the idea of prayer. Talking to God seems entirely credible to a four-year-old, even though the Almighty can't be seen and doesn't say anything himself. Indeed, children chat away to God as to a familiar friend. 'Dear God…', their prayers often begin. Sadly, the questions and doubts come later; yet the memory of prayer remains with most of us. As someone has wisely remarked, there are no atheists in a lifeboat. At some time or other, at moments when we have exhausted every human resource, most if not all of us turn to prayer. When we can't possibly know what the future holds, we bring into the equation someone who we think might do: God.

The veteran broadcaster Rabbi Lionel Blue tells a story of a Jewish man of feeble faith who had the misfortune to slip over the edge of a cliff. As he fell to certain death, he grabbed at a weed growing out of the rock and for a moment hung there. In panic he cried out, 'Oh God, if there be a God, help me now!' To his utter surprise, a voice thundered from the sky. 'Yes, my son. I exist. And here is what you must do. Let go of that weed, and I will send my angels to catch you, lest you dash your head on the rocks below.' For a moment the man hung there silently, then uttered a second cry: 'Is there anybody else?' Jewish storytellers don't spoil things by pointing out the moral, but I shall: you don't have to believe in God in order to pray, but for prayer to 'work' it must surely involve at least a grain of faith on our part as well as God's action in response.

Prayer is natural, then, although it seems a completely irrational thing to do – addressing someone we can't see and who never says anything back to us. Presumably we do it because, somewhere deep down in what we are as humans, there is a conviction, or hope, that there is more to life than meets the eye. Even our super-confident, technologically powered modern society from time to time confronts situations which are utterly beyond its control. The tsunami at the end of 2004 was a powerful example. More commonly, so is the phenomenon we call death. Faced with such things, we tend to seek a power beyond our own and a wisdom beyond technology. If, in addition, we cherish the belief (or the hope) that that power and wisdom is also loving and may operate for our good, then the attraction of prayer becomes irresistible.

To say prayer is 'natural', however, is not at all the same as saying that it is easy. Often we struggle for words to express our fears and longings. Often we should love to pray but feel remote from the God we wish to address. Sometimes we feel we know so little about him, or are such strangers to the whole business of prayer, that it would be impertinent of us to trouble him. Yet still the longing persists. Almost doggedly, even this rather sceptical and agnostic generation refuses to rule out the possibility that prayer can help us, and those we care about.

Many churches have a board near the door where people can write out prayer requests, which are regularly taken down and incorporated in the prayers of a group or a congregation. It is astonishing to see how many people use these; many, if not most of them, not regular churchgoers. Similarly, larger churches and cathedrals often have a candle rack, where people can light a candle as a silent act of prayer. We have one in our cathedral in Oxford, and by mid-morning it will be full of lighted candles. When I am on duty there I like to stand near it so that people can, if they wish, turn to me and tell me why they have lit a candle, or for whom. 'I lit it for my sister, who's ill.' 'I lit it in memory of my best friend, who died last year.' 'I lit it for the children orphaned in the Asian floods.' The reasons are many and varied, but in every case the act of lighting a candle is a form of inarticulate prayer – when we can't find words, then an action can express our intention, and if God can hear our prayers then presumably he can also see our actions.

One way we can find help in prayer is, of course, to use the prayers of others, especially those prayers which have stood the test of time or have proved a source of comfort or strength to other people. The prayers in this book have been chosen simply and solely because they are 'favourite' prayers, ones which thousands and perhaps millions of people have prayed before us. But they can still become, for those who use them, 'our prayers', which as individuals in need we bring to 'our Father in heaven'.

2

God and Prayer

'God help me'

'Prayer is the contemplation of the facts of life from the highest point of view.'

Ralph Waldo Emerson, *Self-Reliance*

I have already said that we don't have to believe in God to pray; but that for prayer to be effective may require faith on our part as well as God's action. That probably needs a little more consideration, because it is a fact of life that in various situations people without conventional faith have prayed and their prayer appears to have been answered.

I think of an instance in the experience of John McCarthy, the British journalist who was held hostage in Beirut during the 1980s. He was at the time in solitary confinement and he later wrote of the fears evoked by that experience in the book *Some Other Rainbow*, which he wrote with Jill Morrell.

> One morning these fears became unbearable. I stood in the cell sinking into despair. I felt that I was literally sinking,

being sucked down into a whirlpool. I was on my knees, gasping for air, drowning in hopelessness and helplessness. I thought that I was passing out. I could only think of one thing to say – 'Help me please, oh God, help me.' The next instant I was standing up, surrounded by a warm bright light. I was dancing, full of joy. In the space of a minute, despair had vanished, replaced by boundless optimism.

McCarthy went on to question what had happened, describing himself as someone who had 'never had any great faith'. He felt he ought to give thanks, but to what, or whom? 'Unsure of the nature of the experience, I felt most comfortable acknowledging the Good Spirit which seemed to have rescued me.' We might wonder whether the very act of crying out for God's help is in itself an 'act of faith'. In any case, McCarthy's experience, which could be replicated over and over again in the lives of countless people, reassures us that answered prayer is not a reward for the pious but the gift of a generous God.

So in what sense do prayer and faith mix? The Bible says that 'whoever would approach [God] must believe that he exists and that he rewards those who seek him' (Hebrews 11:6). I suppose that even McCarthy's prayer, wrung from him in the depths of despair, was an indication of belief, if not in the clearly defined God of the creed, then at least in a 'Good Spirit' who can 'rescue' us. That may be the tiny grain of faith which Jesus himself said is all that is necessary to move mountains (Mark 11:23). In order to pray, we don't need to pass some test of orthodoxy. Perhaps the chief requirement is a deep and true longing for our prayer's fulfilment.

However, having said all that, most people would recognize that prayer involves God, at least in the sense of a benign power who can hear our prayer and do something about it. Although sometimes it may feel like it, we don't pray to the pillow, the sofa or the ceiling. Someone has to hear and act on our request. I think of the line in the old song by the Bachelors, 'I Believe': 'I believe that someone in the great somewhere hears every word.' That is about as vague as belief can get! It may not be essential for the one who prays to know the precise identity of the one to whom they pray, but it is surely necessary that they recognize that prayer is the very opposite of self-help. Prayer humbles us, because in effect we are saying 'I can't, but you can.' It may be that very element in prayer that makes it seem more difficult for modern people, and also for men rather than women. We shall not pray effectively if we retain a vestige of an idea that we could, at a pinch, do it all ourselves. It was that utter despair, that total casting of the burden on the other, which is so startlingly real in John McCarthy's account. At the end of ourselves, we find that there is not a void, but divine love. That is the great secret of prayer.

Many people have little difficulty in believing in God as 'first cause': as the power and wisdom behind creation. However, that notion of God seems far removed from the concept of 'divine love' I have just mentioned: the love of a God who can hear my prayer and enter intimately into my concerns and needs. The opening chapter of the Bible presents a powerful picture in story and metaphor of the creator at work. 'Let there be light', he thunders, 'and let there be sky and earth and water. And let there be creatures in the water, and then on the land and in the sky. And – eventually – let there be people, men and women, to live on the earth and care for it.'

Yet even in this picture of boundless cosmic energy and creative power there is concern for what God has made. The man and the woman are 'made in his image': sharing the divine nature, self-conscious, morally autonomous, capable of love and loyalty yet free to reject them. They are set in a garden of delights, with abundant food, beauty and innocent love. This is not the picture of a cosmic dynamo pumping energy into an empty universe, but of a God who is both powerful and personal, who in the most intimate details of life cares for his creatures. That, as the story of the Bible unfolds, is the God who hears and answers prayer.

All of this, of course, might be taken to refer mainly to prayer in its most common aspect – prayer as most of us think of it – prayer as *request*. But prayer is so much more than that. In a human relationship, there would be something disturbingly abnormal if the only communication were in terms of asking and receiving (and especially if the direction were permanently one way). If the *only* time we pray is when we want something desperately, we have reduced our relationship to God to a series of 999 calls. I am sure they 'get through', and because he is a generous and loving God he may deal kindly with them, but that is no basis for a lasting relationship of trust. Prayer, in other words, comes best from those who have learnt a way of conversing with God, not only about our needs, but about our feelings, about our relationship with him, about seeking to know what *he* wants rather than endlessly what we want. Our next chapter, on the world's best-known prayer, picks up that theme.

3

The Lord's Prayer

'Our Father'

**❛How ready is heaven
to those that pray!❜**

Ben Johnson, *Volpone*

Our Father, who art in heaven, hallowed be thy name.
Thy Kingdom come, thy will be done, on earth as it is in
heaven.
Give us this day our daily bread,
And forgive us our trespasses, as we forgive those who
trespass against us.
And lead us not into temptation, but deliver us from evil.
For thine is the kingdom, the power and the glory, for ever
and ever. Amen.

Every day throughout the world literally millions of people pray
this prayer. It rises in thousands of languages and dialects from the
lips of young and old, men and women, intellectuals and
illiterates. It knows no barriers of race, caste, colour or social class.
Indeed, its very first words emphasize its universality: *'Our*

Father'. This is a prayer addressed by the children of the creator to the one they recognize as the Father of every human being.

In fact it is doubtful if Jesus, who first spoke this prayer to his disciples, intended it to become a form of words to be employed over and over again in a uniform way for ever and ever. 'When you pray, pray *in this way*,' he told them – not necessarily *in these words*. So it is, in effect, a pattern for all prayer, rather than a form of words to be employed; though there can be no harm in repeating them, of course. In this prayer Jesus sets out the principles which underlie all praying – indeed, principles which shape every approach to God. So, while many of us will still want to pray the words of this prayer regularly, we may also find in its pattern a shape and guide for all our other prayers, especially in its clear sense of spiritual priorities.

The first of those priorities is God himself. The prayer is addressed to a heavenly 'Father'. Evidence suggests that when Jesus himself prayed he used the intimate word *abba* for father, rather than a more formal title. *Abba* is an Aramaic word which appears a couple of times in the Greek text of the New Testament, and is nearer the English 'dad' or even 'daddy' than the formal Greek word *pater*, meaning the head of the family. *Abba* would be the name on the lips of a child climbing on to its father's lap; a word which speaks of love and security. How appropriate, then, to start our prayers by reminding ourselves that the God we are addressing is both the great creator of the universe, but also the one we can think of as a gentle, loving and trustworthy parent.

Of course not all human fathers are loving and trustworthy, and over the years I have met many people for whom this has raised problems even in prayer to God. They find it hard to equate the notion of 'father' to these gentle qualities and hence find fatherly language about God unhelpful. If our personal experience of a father has been painful, even abusive, it is very difficult to use the title to describe a loving, generous, forgiving and entirely good parent, which is our understanding of the nature of God. In that case, we may feel free to address God in other terms – as Creator God, as saviour, as Lord. But nevertheless we shall need to find a way of relating those titles to the gentle, loving and trustworthy qualities of a good parent if our understanding of God is not to be rather limited.

In the version of the prayer in the Gospel of Matthew, the God we address is our Father 'in heaven' – our heavenly Father as compared to any other. That also, I suppose, may help those who have problems about earthly fathers. However, the real effect of the title is to point the intercessor heavenwards. We are addressing our prayer to one who inhabits eternity and who sees everything, including the concerns of our own lives, from a eternal perspective. This is not an earthbound prayer, limited as we necessarily are by time, space and understanding. It reminds us that the things which occupy our concerns at any given moment are probably transient (though pressing, even painful, at the time). To pray is to begin to see human life, human problems and human relationships through an eternal perspective – if we may put it this way – through the eyes of the creator, who sees the end from the beginning.

As if to emphasize the priority of God, the very first petition in the prayer is that his 'name' should be 'hallowed'. That's a difficult word to translate into modern English. Indeed, the only time it's used nowadays in ordinary speech is in reference to some place of distinction or history – the 'hallowed turf' of Lord's cricket ground, for instance. In fact it means to make something or someone sacred, or to honour them as 'holy'. God's name is to be reverenced because he is holy; in fact, he is the source of all holiness. Whatever is holy comes from God.

The next petition summarizes the whole of the prayer, in effect: 'your kingdom come'. That, also, is not an easy concept for modern people, accustomed to constitutional monarchies where the sovereign has in reality very little power at all. (I believe the Queen can sell the Navy, but that's about it.) In the ancient world a king and a kingdom represented absolute power – power of life and death, of judgment and execution, of legislation and judiciary. The notion of God as 'king' runs right through the Bible and to pray for his 'kingdom' to come is to pray that his absolute rule may hold sway everywhere. However, this is no arbitrary power exercised on a monarch's whim, but a reign of absolute justice and loving care for his people. To enter into God's kingdom is to place oneself voluntarily under the just and generous rule of one who wants only the best for his children.

We next pray that God's will may be done, which seems to imply that it might not be in some circumstances. In fact, where the creation is concerned, his will is absolute. As the Bible says, 'He spoke and it was done.' Yet there is an exception within his creation, and it concerns us – human beings. Alone in that creation, so far as we know, we have been given what can only be called 'moral autonomy': the fearful right to decide whether to do right or wrong; the awesome responsibility of choice. By his own will God has given us the liberty to reject that will; but also the liberty to pray that we don't.

'Your kingdom come' and 'your will be done' seem to be two ways of saying much the same thing, which is to reinforce the priority of God's will in prayer. Prayer, as we shall consider later, is not a matter of me trying to persuade God to do what I want, but me cooperating with God in what *he* wants. That's a crucial distinction, underlined by these elements of the Lord's Prayer, so easily said, and yet so difficult to comprehend.

The next petition, however, seems much more straightforward: 'Give us this day our daily bread'. It's a request to God to meet our needs – the 'bread for today', like the manna that fell each night on the Israelite camp as they travelled from slavery in Egypt to freedom in the Promised Land. Sometimes this prayer has a particular relevance. I think of a Ugandan family I met in London, who had survived the civil war following the rule of President Amin. Their village shop had been destroyed and often they literally didn't know where the next meal was to come from. Each day at family prayers they prayed 'Give us this day our daily bread' – 'and, do you know,' I was told, 'he did'. It was not luxury, but it was always just enough, until, eventually, the war was over, the village shop was rebuilt and the lorries ran regularly again.

There follows a petition which links God's forgiveness of us with our willingness to forgive others. In one version the failures are 'debts', and in another simply 'sins' (certainly no mention of 'trespasses' in the modern sense of the word). Again, one version implies that unless we are willing to forgive, we can't expect to be forgiven while the other simply links them together – 'forgive us our sins, for we ourselves forgive' (Luke 11:4). The heart of the matter is quite simple, though: those who find it hard to forgive will find it hard to be forgiven – and experience of life bears that out. Sometimes it is as hard to accept forgiveness as it is to give it, for both require us to face up to the reality of anger, jealousy and moral failure in human experience.

The last request has also caused problems, but mainly over translation. The version traditionally said in church reads 'lead us not into temptation', which seems to imply that God *might*, in some circumstances, do just that. The problem there is that in another book of the New Testament, James, the writer (who may have been a brother or cousin of Jesus) warns categorically that we should never say, 'I am being tempted by God,' for 'God cannot be tempted by evil and he himself tempts no one' (James 1:13).

However, recent versions of the Bible translate the phrase in the Lord's Prayer as referring not to 'temptation' but to 'testing': 'Do not put us to the test' or 'Do not bring us to the time of trial'. God does allow us to be tested (again, an everyday experience of life), but that is not the same as being tempted to do evil. In any case, the prayer is a balanced one, because it continues, 'but rescue us from evil' (or, 'the evil one'). The apostle Paul referred to exactly this experience in one of his letters. 'No testing has overtaken you that is not common to everyone,' he wrote. 'God is faithful, and he will not let you be tested beyond your strength, but with the testing he will also provide the way out so that you may be able to endure it' (1 Corinthians 10:13). The language of the apostle is very specific and careful. God does not directly 'test' us, or put us to the test, but he permits us to be tested, whether by circumstances, other people or, perhaps, that strange being the Bible calls 'Satan' (adversary). It is precisely that 'testing', a common experience of human life, which this petition in the Lord's Prayer is addressing. When we are under pressure, God is with us. When we feel we are being put to the test, he stands by us. When we feel we cannot cope, he can give us the strength to do so – a 'way out so that you may be able to endure it'.

Traditionally the prayer has ended with an ascription of glory to God, which can be found in some early manuscripts of the Gospels, though not in the oldest ones: 'For the kingdom, the power and the glory are yours, for ever and ever.' In this way we recognize that the object of our prayer is the coming of God's kingdom; the power that can answer our prayers and bring in that kingdom is his; and the fulfilment of our prayers will be both human joy and divine glory.

From all of this we can see that the Lord's Prayer, for all its apparently childlike simplicity, is in fact a prayer of profound spiritual meaning and experience. It has three clear sections, which we could use to shape our own private prayers. First, there is the holiness of God, our heavenly Father, the pre-eminence of his will and a longing for the coming of his 'kingdom'. Then there is our need for daily provision, not simply of food but of every necessary thing for life. And lastly there is the vital matter of our own spiritual welfare: forgiveness, strength and help. Patterned in that way, our prayers will always follow the divine priorities.

The disciples asked, 'Lord, teach us to pray' – and he gave them this pattern prayer. As we make its pattern our own, we enrol ourselves in Christ's 'school of prayer' and begin to learn from him not *what* to pray, but – more importantly – *how* to pray.

4

How, When and Where to Pray

Private, public, uttered or unexpressed

‘There are moments when,
whatever be the attitude of
the body, the soul is on
its knees. ’

Victor Hugo, *Saint Denis*

If we could wing our way secretly around the city and peep into homes, churches, temples, mosques, gardens and even bedrooms, in one place we might see a man with arms aloft, declaiming loudly towards the ceiling. There might be another man wearing a dark brown cloak, walking silently in a walled garden, lips apparently sealed. There might be a room full of people who seem to be chattering noisily, though we can detect no known tongue that they are speaking. There might be another group holding books and reciting words together, obviously following a set form. And there might be a mother seated by a child's cot, speaking quietly but probably unheard by the toddler who appears to be soundly asleep.

There seems little in common between their activities, and yet every one of these people is in one form or another engaged in the same thing: prayer. Such (and more) are its many faces. These (and many others) are pathways to the presence of God. The monk in the garden is no more profoundly at prayer than the mother praying by the sleeping form of a beloved child. The group praying in tongues is on a different pathway to the same presence as the congregation following a set liturgy. The man with arms aloft is reciting his daily prayers, not to the ceiling, of course, but to God the all-merciful. That each individual and group is praying cannot be denied, despite the obvious differences of content, style, posture and location. The sublime truth is that there are no 'right' or 'wrong' ways to pray, so long as we are seeking to address the one true recipient of all our prayers, the infinite and loving God who hears.

Yet it's worth considering the many different forms that prayer may take, if only to reassure ourselves that our own pathway of prayer is authentic and real. I am often asked, 'Is it all right to...?' – and there follow any number of hesitations about prayer. Is it all right to pray for my cat? Is it all right if I pray standing up, or lying down, or sitting, or while I'm driving the car or even, bizarrely, swimming? I think my answer to each of them is 'yes', with the qualification that prayer while driving is best done with the eyes open.

Yet of course how we pray does affect our own understanding and appreciation of what we are doing, even if it makes little or no difference to God. I may feel comfortable and at home with liturgical prayer but uneasy with a group praying in tongues. That probably means that while I should not force myself to do what I find uncomfortable, nevertheless I might contemplate the possibility that my life of prayer has become rather cosy and may need the shock of being with people praying in tongues to disturb it in a creative kind of way. I may find it a warm and bonding experience to pray at an infant's bedside, yet find it almost impossible to relate that to any need for prayer in my own life or for my own concerns. I may find silent prayer isolating and even eccentric but when I turn to public prayer it seems embarrassing. Where and how we pray, in other words, tells us a great deal about ourselves and our own relationship (or lack of it) with God. To enlarge the ways in which we pray, the forms and words we use, even the topics we bring to God, can not only revolutionize our approach to prayer, but our understanding of the sort of people we are, and the nature of the God we seek to approach.

Most of us think of prayer in terms of a private contact with divine power. I am constantly surprised at the number of people I meet who pray privately but regularly, even though they seldom if ever go to church and pray with others. Often they will admit that their prayers are simple and brief, sometimes shaped around a form of words taught to them as children – a night-time blessing, a placing of loved ones into God's care, a prayer for quiet sleep and a peaceful life. Of course, in times of need those prayers will be supplemented. A child or grandchild's illness will stir us to pray, as may a public crisis or a tragic event in the news. There are still many, many people in our modern and outwardly secular society who would no sooner go to sleep without 'saying their prayers' than they would without cleaning their teeth.

Many of these prayers are said well tucked up under the bedclothes, though there are still people who kneel by their bedside to pray. In fact, the posture of prayer (kneeling, standing, sitting, walking, lying down) is no longer regarded even by most devoutly religious people as very important, though it has to be said it is for Muslims. The old Anglican Prayer Book stipulated that the general confession should be said by the congregation 'meekly kneeling upon their knees' – though what else Archbishop Cranmer thought they could kneel on is hard to imagine. Modern Christian congregations, however, may be found standing, sitting or kneeling for prayer, the practice varying usually according to culture and tradition.

Of course, bodily posture in any activity is important, partly because it tells us how profoundly it is engaging us. Slouching or slumped in a sofa would not seem an appropriate attitude for a deeply penitent sinner to adopt when seeking forgiveness, for instance. Sometimes our hands, which we use so effectively in an animated conversation, can also express our prayers: lifted up in praise to God; clasped in concentration; opened to receive a gift or blessing. But no one should feel that their prayer is disqualified because they can't stand or kneel or sit to do it. 'The saints praise thee upon their beds,' sang the psalmist; we may assume they were still awake while they were doing it.

The time at which we pray may also be important. For instance, praying just before we sleep – which is a very common practice – runs the danger that we may actually fall asleep while doing it. Early-morning prayer, which avoids that problem, is difficult for many because of domestic and family complications. Some people I know choose to pause for prayer at lunch-time, even during a working day, which provides a kind of spiritual interval in the business of life.

Probably the most important thing for those who wish to take prayer seriously is to have a more or less *regular* time, a kind of rendezvous with God. This is not because of his unavailability at other times, but because of our own forgetfulness and carelessness. If we pray when the mood strikes us we may find that we only pray when the immediate need presses, which is quite a different matter. So morning, noon or night doesn't matter, but prayer is surely too important an element of life to leave to human whim. If we arrange a time in our own minds we can, under pressure of circumstances, alter it without feeling guilty. If we have no regular time, we may go for days or weeks without realizing that prayer has slipped right out of our daily agenda.

There is a question in many people's minds about the relative value of private or corporate prayer. Jesus clearly regarded private prayer as important. 'Whenever you pray,' he told his disciples, 'go into your room and shut the door and pray to your Father who is in secret; and your Father who sees in secret will reward you' (Matthew 6:5–6). Of course, the context of this advice was a warning against people who paraded their piety by praying at street corners 'so that they may be seen by others'. That's not a major problem in our society! However, his words do emphasize the value of the quiet place and the personal, private conversation with God.

At the same time, Jesus taught his followers to pray together. In fact, he added a promise to the advice, that 'if two of you agree… about anything you ask, it will be done for you by my Father in heaven'. He also gave the reasoning behind the promise: 'For where two or three are gathered in my name, I am there among them' (Matthew 18:19-20). In other words, there is a further element to prayer when we share in it with others. Not only do we have the benefit of others' understanding of people and situations, but together we can share the presence of Christ as we pray. I would say that for many people the moment when they learnt to pray simply and spontaneously with someone else, or with a small group of friends, was when prayer really came alive.

All of this requires a degree of personal discipline – at least enough of it to create a space in our lives for prayer. It is the absence of time that many people give as a reason for not praying regularly. However, it would be wrong to end this chapter without saying that emergency prayer is also both valid and valuable. Some people refer to these as 'arrow prayers' – a quick referring of an urgent problem or situation to the God who constantly listens.

There's a lovely example in the Bible, when a cupbearer to the king of Persia, a man called Nehemiah, was suddenly given the opportunity to make a request to the monarch on behalf of his exiled Jewish fellow-countrymen. The king had seen that he was troubled about something and asked him what it was. Nehemiah explained that his home city, Jerusalem, lay in waste while its residents were exiled far away. At that the king said to him, 'What do you request?' Nehemiah's account of the incident then goes like this: 'So I prayed to the God of heaven. Then I said to the king...' His 'arrow' prayer must have reached its mark, because his request was granted and eventually led to the rebuilding of Jerusalem and its temple (Nehemiah 2:2-5).

Sometimes in life we have to make an instant decision, or tackle a problem immediately, and that is when the emergency prayer is fully justified. I can imagine the paramedic kneeling by a roadside casualty, or the parent picking up an injured child, praying in just this way. 'God help me' and 'Lord, show me what to do' seem appropriate and adequate prayers for the occasion. Eloquence is hardly required in the circumstances and might even be an unhelpful luxury. We pray... and we act.

Some friends who were on a long pilgrimage across France on foot found themselves stranded miles from anywhere with night drawing in fast. The wife sat at the side of the road and prayed, while her husband stood and thumbed any passing cars for a lift. In fact, it was a deserted country road. The first vehicle to come by was a farm tractor, which was not much help. It was eventually followed by a car with four people in it. As my friend signalled desperately, they waved back in a cheery and encouraging kind of way, but didn't stop. He looked towards his wife and wondered whether he should tell her to stop praying – it evidently wasn't working. However, after a few minutes the same car came back, but now with only two occupants. The waves had been intended to signal that they would return, and now they were in a position to offer a lift right into the nearest town. One could argue for hours whether the wife's prayers or her husband's thumbing were more influential on the happy outcome. The logical conclusion would be that both were part of the same process. Prayer is never a substitute for action, but action without prayer may be wrong-headed and even counter-productive. The crucial element, of course, is neither our words nor our actions, but God's response.

How, when and where we pray are secondary questions. They may affect our feelings about prayer, making it easier or more difficult, but they don't matter much to God. Jesus once corrected a Samaritan woman who wanted to draw him into an argument about the 'correct' place for prayers to be said. He dismissed such questions as fundamentally irrelevant, and then said, 'God is spirit, and those who worship him must worship in spirit and truth' (John 4:20–24). It is not, in other words, a matter of *where*, so much as to *whom*. And as for 'how', the answer of Jesus is very simple: 'in spirit and truth'. Words can't deceive the God who reads hearts and listens more to our deepest desires than to our spoken requests. The old hymn puts it very succinctly: 'Prayer is the soul's sincere desire/Uttered or unexpressed.' It is, after all, the heart that prays.

5

The Many Faces of Prayer

Pathways to the presence of God

‘Nowhere can man find a quieter or more untroubled retreat than in his own soul.’

Marcus Aurelius, *Meditations*

Most people think of prayer as 'asking', but that is only one aspect of prayer, and probably not the most fundamental. Prayer is the connection of the human heart and mind with its creator, and that connection can take place in many different ways, as we shall see in this chapter.

In the first place, it can happen in silence. We live in a relentlessly noisy world, apparently intent on the abolition of silence – every shop, every airport, every café apparently needs to be soaked in an endless flood of recorded music. At home the radio blares in one room, the television in the next and in the study the computer constantly emits irritating jingles. The abolition of silence has several serious consequences, but none greater than the abolition of mental space. We need gaps in our aural landscape for the inner voice to be heard, not least because that may from time to time be the voice of God.

There's a beautiful story in the Bible about the prophet Elijah. He had been hounded by the evil king Ahab and his equally evil wife Jezebel. Most of the faithful prophets of God had been slain by them and Elijah himself was forced to flee into the wilderness for safety. There he had a severe attack of depression, convinced that the righteous cause was lost and that he was the only one left to fight for it: 'and they are seeking my life, to take it away' (1 Kings 19:10).

God brought him to Mount Horeb to shelter in a cave, and there the Lord spoke to him, not in spectacular fashion – shouting at him through the noise of a storm, or thunder and lightning, or an earthquake – though all of them shook the mountain. Instead, Elijah heard the voice of God in what the old translation described as a 'still, small voice' but my modern translation renders more accurately (but more surprisingly) as 'a sound of sheer silence' (1 Kings 19:12). It is in those rare but precious moments of 'sheer silence' that we can often hear the voice of God.

Sometimes it will be the voice of conscience, correcting or rebuking us. Sometimes it will be the voice of encouragement or inner strength. Sometimes it will be the voice of guidance, saying to us, 'this is the way'. Of course we shall need wisdom, or perhaps experience, to be sure that what we are hearing is the voice of God, and not simply that of our own wishes and desires. We can test it against God's known and revealed standards as we find them in the biblical commandments or the teaching of Jesus. Our conscience wouldn't, for instance, guide us to do something selfish, deceitful or self-indulgent. We can also test what we 'hear' by discussing what we believe he has said to us with a wise pastor, friend or counsellor.

Whatever the message or its meaning, it will be best received by us in silence, or as near silence as we can manage. One of the great attractions of the growing retreat movement is that it offers to people a place and a structure in which silence is not odd, but normal. Kahlil Gilbran writes of this mystery of the inner voice in his book *The Prophet*:

The veil that clouds your eyes shall be lifted by the hands
that wove it. And the clay that fills your ears shall be
pierced by those fingers that kneaded it. And you shall
see and you shall hear.

In other words, the God who speaks to us is the God who enables us to hear, even with ears that were previously spiritually deaf.

Silence is certainly one form of prayer, but not by any means the only one. Gratitude is another voice of prayer, and one – if I may put it like this – that delights the heart of God. We teach children to say 'thank you', and most of us are quite good at remembering to thank relatives and friends for gifts or parties. Few of us could truthfully claim that we don't like being thanked, especially if we sense real gratitude and pleasure in the gesture. However, God, who according to the Bible is the source of every 'good and perfect gift', is liable to be left off our 'thank you' lists. We are mostly far better and more eloquent in making our requests known to him than in expressing gratitude when those requests are met.

Perhaps every time of prayer should begin with such expressions, looking back and reviewing the good things we have been given, what the old prayer calls 'all the blessings of this life'. If we 'count our blessings' in this way, 'it may surprise us what the

Lord has done,' as the hymn says. We are probably not a very grateful generation, more conscious of our supposed needs than of those daily 'blessings', yet as we turn to the source of every blessing it seems appropriate to express our genuine gratitude... before bringing the next list of requests to him!

Another facet of prayer is penitence – again, not a practice that sits comfortably with current styles of thinking. We are suspicious nowadays of the whole notion of 'guilt' and are aware of people whose lives are made miserable by the irremovable burden of it. On the other hand, most of us are conscious that every day we do or say or think things which are wrong and for which, to some degree at least, we feel ashamed. To acknowledge that, and deal with it, is not at all the same as feeding a 'guilt complex'. As we draw near to God, who is 'the source of all holiness', we shall inevitably become more aware of such failings. Recognizing our faults and confessing them frankly to God is not a negative experience but, as millions have discovered, a deeply liberating one. After all, 'if we confess our sins, he who is faithful and just will forgive us our sins and cleanse us from all unrighteousness' (1 John 1:9). Penitence, rightly understood, is a true pathway into the presence of God.

Having earlier mentioned prayer as a means of seeking God's guidance, it is also important to think about prayer as 'enquiry' or a 'search'. The Bible frequently puts these words in the mouth of God: 'If you truly seek me, you will find me.' Undoubtedly prayer is part of the seeking process. It is also part of the sometimes more complicated process of determining God's will, as distinct from our own.

There is a vivid example of this in the life of Jesus. On the evening of his betrayal and arrest he is at prayer in the Garden of Gethsemane. 'In an agony', the Gospels record, he prays to his

Father to 'remove this cup' (the cup of suffering and death) away from him. However, he adds the crucial qualifying words, 'yet, not my will but yours be done' (Luke 22:42). There is the perfect prayer of 'enquiry'. Jesus, as a human being, no more relished the idea of crucifixion than we would, so he asked his Father and God whether it was possible for that fate to be avoided; was there, in effect, a 'Plan B' for the salvation of the world? But almost in the same breath he also acknowledged that his Father knew what was best and what had to be done: 'yet, not my will but yours'. So much of our praying, and so many of our problems about prayer, would be transformed if we could learn those sacred and profound words.

Finally, as we consider the many faces of prayer, there is the one which we find most conspicuously in the Hebrew Psalter: praise and adoration. The psalmist constantly bursts into songs of praise: 'I will exalt you, my God and king;' 'I will praise the name of God with a song; I will magnify him with thanksgiving;' 'Blessed be the Lord, the God of Israel, who alone does wondrous things. Blessed be his glorious name for ever; may his glory fill the whole earth. Amen and amen.'

For some people this raises problems. What sort of a God is it who needs to be constantly told how wonderful he is? I remember thinking as an eight-year-old choirboy that it was all a bit much – surely even God must get bored with being praised in such exaggerated terms? 'Serenading God' is how one cynic described it.

However, such criticisms rather miss the point. Human praise of God is not designed to tell him something he doesn't already know, but to express how we feel about him. When the besotted young man gazes into the eyes of his girlfriend and says 'Darling, you're so beautiful', he isn't making a cool judgment of her qualities (the shape of her mouth, the set of her jaw, the alignment of her eyes) so much as revealing how he feels about her. To praise God is not to inform him but to inspire ourselves: the One we worship is altogether worthy of it. He has shown in many ways that he loves us, not least by giving his Son to die for us. In our praise and worship we try to show him something of the love which we feel in response. As the apostle John writes, 'We love because he first loved us' (1 John 4:19).

To express praise may be natural enough – look at a football crowd roaring their 'worship' of the team! – but where prayer is concerned, and especially private prayer, it can feel awkward and stilted. We may be all right singing 'Praise, my soul, the king of heaven' in a large congregation, and even find it moving and inspiring, but it may be different when we try to introduce the element of worship and adoration into our own prayers. Of course, if at that moment we are feeling very grateful about something, then it will be easier to say so: gratitude and praise are at least close cousins. But without that kind of incentive we may find ourselves mouthing what sound like well-worn slogans rather than spontaneous praise and adoration.

Time then to turn to the book of Psalms! Let someone else put words into your mouth; not slogans, but the well-honed thoughts and words of those who have gone before us with faith in the same God. Just as we might use a Shakespearean sonnet to express how we feel about someone we love, so we may use others' words to express our praise and adoration of the creator. Once the verbal pump is primed, as it were, we may find that our own words of praise and adoration follow quite naturally.

We can't make God greater than he is, however much we praise him, but our praise can lift us up to where he is. If adoration, worship and praise are indeed the chief occupations of heaven, as the book of Revelation strongly suggests, then it might be no bad idea to get in some practice now.

As the poet George Herbert put it,

In my heart, though not in heaven, I can raise thee.
Small it is, in this poor sort to enrol thee:
E'en eternity's too short to extol thee.

6

Problems with Prayer

The questions people ask

🍂 Unanswered prayer

There was a teenage girl at the back of the church looking
miserable. I remarked that she looked as though she'd lost a five-
pound note. Her response took me by surprise, 'I'm off God at the
moment.' As vicars are supposed to do, I asked in precisely what
ways the Almighty had incurred her displeasure. She explained
that she and a friend at school had been praying, *really* hard, for
this friend's mother, who had cancer, but she'd died. 'What's the
point in praying,' she asked, 'if he doesn't take any notice?'

That incident crystallized a common problem about prayer:
what people call 'unanswered' prayer. I put it like that because
it isn't necessarily unanswered at all: it may be that God's

answer is 'No'. God, who knows everything, past, present and future, also knows what is right for us and those for whom we pray. And sometimes what is right for us, or others, isn't what we are asking for.

The Bible is well aware of the problem. In the letter of James it says, 'You do not have, because you do not ask. You ask and do not receive, because you ask wrongly, in order to spend what you get on your pleasures' (James 4:2–3). It can't be denied that sometimes our prayers are not much more than wish lists, the sort of thing we wrote to Father Christmas as children.

That seems obvious enough in some cases: the youngster praying for a mountain bike; the politician praying to win an election; a candidate praying to pass an important examination. What they are asking for is not necessarily wrong in itself, but the motive has a ring of selfishness about it. However, it's also true that apparently unselfish prayers may spring from mixed motives. To pray that an elderly relative should go on living because we would miss them so much were they to die could also be selfish. God may know that their ultimate good outweighs our sense of personal deprivation.

All of that, however, is no answer to my disillusioned teenage friend. What could be more natural than prayer that a relatively young woman, the mother of a couple of children, should recover from a serious illness? Equally, what could be less selfish than praying that wars and famines would end in far-off lands, or that innocent people would be protected from terrorist attacks or natural disasters? And people do pray for those things, endlessly, yet they endlessly happen. Is God not listening? Does he not care? Or – a terrible thought – is he, too, powerless to do anything about it?

There are no simple answers to questions like those. One can say truthfully that from time to time people are miraculously healed in answer to prayer. In my life I can think of one incontrovertible example, but only one. One can say that many of the evils which we pray to be delivered from are the products of human sin, and that God by his own decision and will has made human beings in such a way that they are 'free' to sin. Part of the glory and the risk of being human is the fearful right to say 'No' to God. He has made us that way and he will not overrule our God-given right to decide, even if that decision is contrary to his will. Even our prayers can't make an unrepentant person repent. Prayer isn't magic, a spell which we can cast on people to make them do what we want, even if what we want is clearly God's will. So some prayer is 'unanswered' because for God to answer it would be to take away someone's moral responsibility.

That leaves far the most difficult area of so-called 'unanswered' prayer, which is concerned with protection from famine, earthquake, cancer and other devastating things which occur in human experience and cause enormous sadness, pain and loss. Again, there's no simple answer, but it is fair to say that prayer cannot change the way the world is. That is to say, other than in totally exceptional circumstances, our prayers are unlikely to persuade God to alter or interfere with the normal physical laws of the universe he has created.

If I am trying to fix a roof tile and fall over the edge, the law of gravity (which normally keeps me safely fixed to the ground) determines that I shall travel suddenly, speedily, painfully and possibly even fatally to the ground below. I should not (again, in the normal course of events) expect God to send a couple of angels to catch me before I hit the ground, regardless of how many people have been praying for my safety. We live in an ordered universe whose creator appears reluctant to interfere with that natural order. Indeed, the consequence of his doing so could itself be calamitous!

That is not say, of course, that he *couldn't*, or that he never has, but that all the evidence of the Bible, of experience and of common sense tells us that he usually *doesn't*. Chance and accident are part of the way things are, the way the world is – which is much the same as saying that they are part of the way God has made things.

None of this means that we should not pray for people who are ill, or for protection for our loved ones, or for an end to human greed and sin. The truth is that God operates in that world, often in response to prayer, not necessarily to change the way things are but to change the way we see them or others experience them. Even when our prayers don't alter circumstances, in other words, they can and do give strength to us and others to live in the world as it is with a loving God alongside us.

❧ Why pray at all?

Perhaps an even more fundamental problem than unanswered prayer is one which is very much the product of our modern way of thinking: not 'how' does God deal with our prayers but 'why should anyone pray?' For that matter, why should God bother with prayer? He knows what is right and good and just. He has infinite power (or what's the point in being God at all?). So why doesn't he simply *do* it?

This raises the fascinating question as to the role of prayer. Is it an elaborate and rather sneaky way of getting God to do what we want? There are stories in the Old Testament which seem to point that way (read Genesis 18:22–33, for instance, though the balance of Scripture would suggest that that is a rather crude reading of a profound and moving encounter between Abraham and his God). Or is it, rather, a kind of empty ritual in which what God wants is done, but we get the warm feeling that somehow we're involved too?

The answer of Scripture and experience is that it's neither; at any rate not in that categorical way. Yes, prayer is about bringing our own needs and longings to God in the hope that he will in some way meet them; and yes, it is a way of involving human beings in bringing about the fulfilment of the will of God. But those two things need not be mutually exclusive. It must be true that God desires the happiness and welfare of his children, and therefore presumably longs to bring it about. He knows, however, as every human parent does, that simply to give in to every request from a child, however demanding, is not to bless them but to spoil them. The process of prayer is one in which two wills come together: God's will for our blessing, and our will to be blessed. Of course, those wills are not 'equal', either in understanding or ability, yet in prayer God has made it possible for our prayers of limited understanding, and our inability to do anything ourselves to answer them, to be part of a process that works for good.

The great physicist and Christian priest John Polkinghorne in his book *Science and Providence* uses the analogy of the laser beam to illustrate the way this process works. 'Laser light is characterized,' he writes, 'by what the physicists call "coherence", that is to say all the oscillations are in phase, perfectly in step with each other. In that way, effects which otherwise might cancel each other out, can instead afford each other the maximum reinforcement. We can truly use the metaphor of God's laser interaction, not to mean an arbitrarily enforced intervention, but as the tuning of divine and human wills to mutual resonance through the collaboration of prayer.'

Seen like this, prayer is the tuning of two forces which are often at loggerheads: the will of God and the rebellious will of his human creatures. When they do coincide, then things actually happen which otherwise might have been hindered or even prevented from happening at all. As we have seen, God will not arbitrarily overrule human freedom of will, which is his supreme gift to our race, even if as a result his own will, for us or for others, is frustrated. Somewhere in that is the key to the mystery of prayer.

There is, I'm glad to say, a simpler way of putting it. When a child asks something of its parent, and the parent (duly weighing up the pros and cons of the situation) decides to give it to them, and the child gratefully receives it, a process of bonding has occurred. The parent's love for the child has been expressed in action. The child's dependence on the adult has been recognized (you can do it, I can't), and in the expressions of happiness and gratitude the two grow even closer together. Often, and very simply, that is exactly what happens when we pray.

❦ How does God hear every prayer?

Two other problems, of a very different nature, are frequently raised on the subject of prayer. The first is an expression of bafflement that God can hear and attend to all the millions of prayers being offered to him, many at the same time. It has to be said that this is a difficulty created largely by thinking of God as a human being, albeit a rather superior one. Yet, beyond that, we live in a world today in which I can pick up a telephone, tap in a few numbers and expect a receiver to ring in Hong Kong, Rwanda or Australia. At a stroke, and through a human construction, I have selected just one out of the billion or so telephones in the world so that I can have a conversation with someone I can't see, may never have met and possibly know nothing at all about. It seems logical that if our computers can do it, the creator of the universe might be able to do it, too, but the other way round (to receive a million messages at once, that is, and sort them out!).

✤ Wandering thoughts

The other difficulty is a much more personal one. Almost everyone who prays is familiar with the problem of wandering thoughts. We feel guilty because, while allegedly in communication with the Almighty, our butterfly minds have flitted off into some trivial by-way of thoughts far removed from the lofty ones we intended to share with him.

There are two pieces of advice about wandering thoughts which I have found helpful myself. The first is, don't worry about them! The fact that at times our grasshopper minds go leaping off into the less sacred areas of life (sport, perhaps, or the garden, or that unexpected bill which has arrived) only tells us that we are human. It is certainly not automatic grounds for guilt. They *may* fall into that area, of course, but we will know if that is so. For the most part they are 'wanderings', no more and no less.

The second piece of advice goes with that one. Turn your wandering thoughts into prayers. What this means in practice is that if, as we are praying, the thought of that awful bill which came in the post today pops into our mind and distracts our intercessions, instead of trying to push it away and get back to holier thoughts, we can simply bring to God our financial anxieties. We can do the same with less menacing topics: the garden (gratitude for the beauty of nature); sport (the joy of physical exercise and friendly competition); and so on. The God who is interested in every part of our lives – not just the 'religious' bits – will certainly not be shocked at such prayers. In any case, as many great saints of his have discovered, he's not easily shocked.

So much for problems in prayer. However, it would be a pity if people thought of prayer as a problem, rather than a privilege and a joy. Of course questions arise about it, both in theory and in practice, but the life of prayer for most believers is not an endless struggle to make sense of it; nor does it seem to most of us a very odd or unnatural thing to do. As an old hymn puts it:

Prayer is the simplest sound we teach
When children learn God's name;
And yet it is the noblest speech
That human lips can frame.

7

Flying on Familiar Wings

Using well-loved and well-worn prayers

> ‘Words without thoughts
> never to heaven go.’
>
> **William Shakespeare,** *Hamlet*

Sometimes people say to me, 'I'd like to pray, but I don't know what words to use,' as though prayer were a sort of 'abracadabra' to open the gates of heaven. Others say that they would pray, but feel that almighty God sitting in heavenly splendour deserves something better than their halting and clumsy phrases. In truth, prayer is not a magic password and neither is it a kind of celestial examination in literary style. God isn't swayed by our eloquent words, but by the honesty of our intention and the need of our circumstances. 'God help me – I'm scared stiff and I don't know what to do' is probably more likely to touch the heart of the Almighty than the most beautiful and eloquent prayer ever framed.

Nevertheless, and having said that, most of us would like, at least sometimes, to send our prayers flying to heaven on familiar and beautiful wings, rather than scramble there with our own unaided but awkward words. A familiar prayer is like a comfortable pair of old shoes: it enables us to get there with a minimum of fuss and strain. Excused from the struggle to find words, the path to God may seem slightly easier to navigate, especially if within the familiar form are enfolded our honest longings and deepest needs. The true prayer of the heart is the one God longs to hear, because it has an authentic beauty which is unique to the moment. But at times the true prayer of the heart may tap into a universal longing, a shared experience or need, and find in well-tuned phrases and appropriate images just the language which liberates us from the need for spontaneous speech.

This is often particularly true of certain categories of prayer. We may find it easier to express praise and adoration, or regret or penitence, in words which generations of Christians have found appropriate and helpful. Many have found the 'Jesus Prayer' – 'Lord Jesus Christ, Son of God, have mercy on me, a sinner' – a wonderful path into both repentance and praise. The ancient Greek *Kyrie* – 'Lord have mercy, Christ have mercy, Lord have mercy' – may equally provide a way of expressing dependence, sorrow for sin and trust in divine mercy, all in the space of nine words. The anxious person spending a night alone in a strange and perhaps daunting environment may find those ancient words of the Evening Collect a source of comfort and strength: 'Lighten our darkness, Lord, we pray...' And if praise and gratitude are what we wish to express, how could it be better done than in the words of the *Gloria*: 'Glory to God in the highest, and peace to his people on earth. Lord God, heavenly king, almighty God and Father, we worship you, we give you thanks, we praise you for your glory.'

There is no need for us to feel that such prayers are in some way 'second-hand' and therefore lacking in authenticity. It is our heart's intention that gives authenticity to our prayers rather than the language in which they are framed. To have in our minds or even on our bedside table or our bookshelf a veritable mine of devotion is to be able to draw on spiritual riches, riches which become our own as we use them, perhaps over and over again.

In my own experience, what I might call spontaneous prayer is the 'default option', but every day it is supported and balanced by the 'given' prayers of the church. I use the *Daily Office* – *Morning Prayer*, or the Franciscan 'Celebrating Common Prayer'. I also use prayers from many other sources, some remembered by heart, some turned to in a well-worn book. Whether I am praying *extempore* or from favourite texts, I am praying to the same heavenly Father, through the same Jesus Christ and guided in my prayers by the same Holy Spirit. The words I use – my own, or someone else's – are simply the raw material of prayer. Its heart is my own faith, however feeble or tottering, and the genuine intentions of my heart.

All the same, there is something quite inspiring about using words and phrases of beauty, hewn out of the lexicon of other people's long experience of God and the pathway of prayer. After all, I am not the first person to feel alone, or isolated, or sad, or joyful; not the first to need beyond anything else help and succour from a source beyond myself and greater than I can summon up from my own meagre resources. It is a kind of spiritual arrogance to ignore this heritage of prayer, rather like a hungry person refusing to eat a meal because they haven't prepared it themselves.

It is in fact a privilege to draw water from so deep a well. Many streams of experience and faith have fed it, and it can safely be said that no one ever came up dry from its depths.

8

Coming Late to Prayer

For those who need to get started

❝More things are wrought
by prayer than this world
dreams of.❞

Alfred Lord Tennyson,
The Passing of Arthur

Most people recognize, especially at times of stress or danger, that prayer could make an enormous difference to their lives. They may hope, even expect, to find through prayer a calmness and serenity that a few others have but most of us seem to lack. Perhaps when they walk through an ancient place of prayer like a cathedral or a monastery they can capture for a moment that atmosphere of peace and tranquillity, and even sense that it's linked in some way with the prayers that have been offered there.

Yet at other times people may say they are 'too busy' to pray. In all the pressure of everyday life it seems an irrelevance, an indulgence or a luxury. It's this feeling that probably presents modern day people with the biggest disincentive to prayer. Yes, it may be a good idea, it may help other people, it may even work, but it all sounds serious and time-consuming. Consequently, while almost everyone prays sometimes, very few people make it an important part of their daily lives. The result is that where prayer is concerned we're out of practice, rusty and awkward. We're a bit like a pianist who never practises or a cyclist climbing on a bike for the first time in twenty years. Like any life-skill, prayer is difficult if we seldom put it to use. Prayer needs practice.

The telephone is a wonderful thing. You can use it to talk to friends and family, even on the other side of the world. You can buy things, pay your bills, book a holiday. You can hear the weather forecast and find out the time of the next train to the seaside. Used in those ways, the phone is a life-enhancing resource.

On the other hand, you might have a phone but only use it for emergency calls: fire, police, ambulance. It would be far too time-consuming to look up other numbers, master the technology of the modern phone, or waste time in idle conversation or mere curiosity. You are, I suppose, a phone user, but you are using it in a limited way, simply as a convenience in an emergency. The phone sits there all day long, an unconsidered and disregarded resource, waiting for an emergency to call it into action.

Prayer, for some people, is also a wonderful thing. They use it to talk to God, and to talk to him about their friends, even on the other side of the world. They can use it to examine their lifestyle and priorities and put their personal affairs in order. In the silent spaces of prayer they can hear the voice of God and find out what his purposes are for their lives. Used in those ways, prayer, too, is a life-enhancing resource.

At the same time, there are people whose only recourse to prayer is in an emergency. They know prayer exists, but it sits somewhere in the background gathering dust until a calamity arises and they make a grab for it. It would be wrong to say that they can't get through because they're not regular customers – God is always willing to hear us. Indeed, as we saw earlier, there are examples in the Bible, as there are in everyday Christian experience, of the importance of the 'arrow' prayer, fired in a moment of deep need and straight to the heart of God. However, unfamiliarity with what we might call the 'apparatus' of prayer may make us hesitant to go beyond the immediate situation that prompted the prayer. We have 'used' prayer, but in those circumstances have not even begun to discover the full rewards it offers.

Those rewards are in fact enormous. If we find a greater meaning and satisfaction in prayer we shall also experience a much greater sense of God's involvement in our lives and the lives of those for whom we pray. Events of life will tend to fall into some kind of perspective. Parts of our personality and character that we were previously unaware of will be sparked into life. It's no exaggeration to say that the world itself looks a different place when seen through the lenses of our prayers.

Only when we move into these deeper realms of the human spirit and its divine creator shall we begin to see why for some people prayer is not an added extra but an absolute essential to life.

As we have seen, the first requirement of prayer is belief in God – and a God who hears and responds to our prayers. In one sense that's not a problem for most people. They believe that there is a God and the very act of praying presumes some belief that our prayer is heard and may have some effect. Our faith may be small, but the important factor is not the size of our faith but the greatness of the God in whom that faith is placed, however doubtfully. All the same, we shall find that prayer grows in meaning and importance to us as our faith in God grows: the two things go hand in hand. Prayer nourishes faith and faith responds to prayer.

Prayer is also about our relationship with God. That sounds a strange way to put it, but to pray at all is to recognize that God is personal, rather than a cosmic computer or an elemental source of energy. We don't talk to things, but to people. However, even in normal human relationships we often find it quite hard to talk to someone we don't know or have only just met. As we get to know them better, so conversation flows more easily – we have, as it were, a library of shared memories, interests and concerns which we can draw on.

Where God is concerned, we may start with the premise that he cares about us. Sometimes we may bore or even irritate our friends with our obsessions and worries, but God seems endlessly patient in listening to our complaints and problems. It would be unhelpful, however, to think of prayer simply or even mainly as a means of telling God our troubles. Prayer is conversation with the divine, and a conversation that sounds like a list of problems and complaints barely qualifies for the name at all.

Friends or lovers need to talk to build their relationship. Husbands and wives who don't talk to each other invariably run into relationship difficulties. But that talk cannot be one-sided; and won't be if there is genuine love at work. To love someone is truly to care about their good more than our own, to value them above ourselves. That is the self-giving love of which the Bible speaks; the love celebrated in the wedding service in the exchange of vows: 'All that I am I give to you...'

In prayer we talk to God about what is on our minds. That will include how we feel about him, as well as the things we would like him to do for us. In a love relationship (and that is what we are really talking about) there is a mutuality of concern, even if one partner is much stronger, richer or more experienced than the other. We are not God's equals, but we can know that he loves us without condition, and we can see our own love for him grow as we get to know him better. One of the most satisfying things in life is talking with someone we love, and whom we are sure loves us. That is exactly how prayer is meant to be.

You may feel that it's difficult to have a meaningful conversation with someone who never says anything. That's how many people see prayer. We talk to God and he says nothing back. Yet in fact, according to the Bible, God is speaking to us all the time. It says that he speaks to us through the creation: 'The heavens declare the glory of God' says the Psalmist. As we see the sunset, or a field of flowers, or children playing, the eye of faith hears the creator's voice.

God is also said to speak to us, as we have seen, through our consciences. The apostle Paul said that our conscience either 'accuses' or 'excuses' us. It's a kind of moral health check, alerting us to our standing at any given moment. There can't be many people who have never felt the pang of conscience at an action they have taken or a word they have spoken. Everyone has a conscience, but it can get rusty if it's never used, or distorted if it's constantly fed the wrong information. But when it's working properly, conscience can be the voice of God warning and guiding us. Making time to listen to our conscience and to retune it to God's standards is a very important element in prayer.

Then – again, as we've already seen – God speaks to us through the Bible. In fact, it's often called 'the Word of God'. Many people have felt the benefit of reading part of the Bible, even if it's only a verse or two, before they pray. In that way, God gets the first word, though it's worth adding that experience teaches that he'll probably get the last word as well!

It's not quite true, then, that God never 'says anything'. It is true that we aren't very good at listening. That's a conversational fault with a number of people! However, if we make our times of prayer unhurried and include in them space for silence and to listen to the Bible we shall find that they are not entirely one way. A few pictures of natural scenes or places may help us to see God afresh in what he has made. Silent reflection on our own behaviour may enable our conscience to get a word in edgeways. Between them, quiet, reflection, Bible and conscience should ensure that we never again think of our conversations with God as one-sided.

 Getting Started

To begin to take prayer seriously probably requires a few important decisions about time and space, because praying, except in emergency mode, simply can't be rushed. Prayer can't be squeezed into a life that's already full. That's not to say that you have to have a perfect 'holy place' of quiet to talk to God and listen to him, but it is a fact that a regular life of prayer – the kind of prayer that changes our whole approach to things – does require both time and space. So the first step in taking prayer seriously is to create that time and space.

That may well immediately create difficulties. It's all very well for people who have a room of their own and many opportunities for solitude to draw aside and spend quality time with God. But for many of us peace and quiet are not easily found. There may be children to care for, work and domestic responsibilities to balance, an elderly relative to attend to. Or we may live in a small flat or accommodation we share with others who can't help but invade our space from time to time. We might prefer to pray alone, but at times the only place of privacy is the bathroom or bed. The first may not feel conducive to reflection and prayer; the second may simply serve to create a conflict between mind and body: the one intent on prayer, the other intent on sleep.

For reasons like these it's important to create somewhere, somehow, an 'inner space', a little pool of quietness and reflection inside your own head, as it were. If you can find a time in the day when things are a bit less hectic, even for a few moments, it may offer the opportunity to slip away into this interior place of quiet, our own chapel of prayer.

Of course, ideally there *will* be a place: a bedroom, a seat in the park, a space at the kitchen table with a cup of coffee when the baby is asleep. And in that place we can, in the language of the Psalms, 'wait for God'. It will become for us a sacred spot and a sacred time, not a wearisome duty but a privilege to be cherished and enjoyed day by day.

People have created such sacred spots in the strangest of locations. I know of people who have practised the presence of God in a busy canteen, in an army barracks, on a train going to work or even while walking the pram to the shops. God is everywhere, not just in churches, and he is always ready to meet us 'by appointment', wherever we are. But the appointment is crucial. If we simply hope to find time for prayer, or wait for it to turn up in the process of daily life, we shall almost certainly be disappointed.

When we have created time and space, we need some kind of pattern for prayer. This certainly *doesn't* mean a rigid formula. Nothing kills prayer more quickly than that. Yet our prayer needs shape, or it will simply slip away into wandering thoughts.

The shape can vary, of course. It should try to encompass the main elements of prayer which we have considered: thanksgiving, repentance, petition, reflection, worship. As I've suggested earlier, our prayer will also benefit from even a short Bible reading – perhaps a saying of Jesus or a sentence or two from a psalm – to ensure that our conversation with God is not one-sided. Some people like to start with a formal or 'set' prayer, like the ones in this book. They find that words that have helped many others, perhaps over centuries of Christian experience, to relate to the unseen God, may also help them in the same search. These prayers may help to set an agenda, as it were, and create an atmosphere of faith and openness to him. They get us into the right frame of mind for our own prayers and even, perhaps, may loosen our tongues!

In the 'shape' of prayer we shall also (as we have seen) include penitence – an awareness that we are not really worthy to approach a pure and holy God, and that the nearer we come to him the more we sense that unworthiness. However, he has invited us to come, just as we are, needing forgiveness but aware that it has been promised to those who confess and repent their sins and failures. So we might include a simple act of recollection in which we express our sorrow for past sins, confess them to God and ask for his forgiveness.

The thought of that forgiveness, so often sought, so often given, could well lead us into some prayers of gratitude. It's always a good idea to be as specific as possible, naming the good things we have received over the previous day or two and thanking God for people, events, joys and pleasures. It is from this mood of gratitude that we shall move most easily into our requests, when we ask God for the things that are on our hearts, for others and for ourselves.

I hope all that sounds really simple. Too often prayer has been turned from something easy and natural into something technical and complicated. The apostle Paul described prayer in much simpler terms: 'Do not worry about anything, but in everything by prayer and supplication with thanksgiving let your requests be made known to God. And the peace of God, which surpasses all understanding, will guard your hearts and your minds in Christ Jesus' (Philippians 4:6–7). There it is, in a nutshell: don't worry, pray and be grateful, and the peace of God will be yours.

Prayer is not dreadfully complicated but blissfully simple. Indeed, the first step on the pathway of prayer is to demystify it, to see it for what it is: a conversation with someone who values and loves us, and who seeks our love; someone who can do wonderful things for us, if we will only let him. 'Don't worry', said St Paul – 'don't even worry about prayer'! Prayer is to involve God in the affairs of daily life and all the things that concern us: the way we think, the attitudes we adopt, the dreams we dream. In prayer we cultivate true gratitude, and from the process is born what he calls 'the peace of God': a peace that invades heart and mind and delivers us from anxiety and worry.

That peace is both the key to prayer and its chief reward. When we find it, we have found the true meaning of prayer.

The
Nation's Favourite
Prayers

 The Lord's Prayer

The Lord's Prayer, often also known called the 'Our Father', must surely rank as not only the nation's, but also the world's, favourite Christian prayer. It is unique in its universality – its words are used by Christians of all denominations (and none) on every continent – and in being the prayer that the majority of believers are able to say by heart. The prayer Jesus gave to his disciples can be found in Matthew 6:9–13, and you can read more about its context, meaning and significance in chapter three of this book.

The traditional version of the Lord's Prayer (still said in churches using the 1662 *Book of Common Prayer*) is printed on page 16. However, there are now a number of different translations in common use and a number of contemporary paraphrases have been written with the intention of making this great prayer more 'accessible'. Here is another example which, without the doxology, is closest to that found in the Gospels and continues to be used in the Catholic church today.

> *Our Father, who art in heaven,*
> *Hallowed be thy name;*
> *Thy kingdom come;*
> *Thy will be done;*
> *On earth as it is in heaven.*
> *Give us this day our daily bread.*
> *And forgive us our trespasses,*
> *As we forgive those who trespass against us.*
> *And lead us not into temptation;*
> *But deliver us from evil.*
> *Amen.*

# The Hail Mary

The Hail Mary is one of the oldest and most popular Catholic prayers and is now often said as part of the general intercessions.

The early history of this great prayer (also known as the Ave Maria or Angelic Salutation) is unknown and sources suggest that it 'evolved' in three distinct sections. The early scriptural part takes words from the Gospel of Luke and combines the greetings made to Mary by the Angel Gabriel at the annunciation (Luke 1:28) and by Elizabeth at the visitation (Luke 1:42). This was frequently used in worship from the early Middle Ages, with the next sentence being added in the thirteenth century. The prayer was complete by the time it was incorporated into Catholic liturgy in the fifteenth century.

Hail Mary, full of grace,
The Lord is with thee.
Blessed art thou among women,
And blessed is the fruit of thy womb, Jesus.
Holy Mary, Mother of God,
Pray for us sinners,
Now and at the hour of our death.
Amen.

❧ Make Me an Instrument of Your Peace

The son of a wealthy cloth merchant, Francis answered God's call to rebuild the ruined church of San Damiano in Assisi, initially using some family money to do so. Shortly afterwards he adopted a life of poverty and was joined in his rebuilding work by seven men, thus forming the first of what was to become the order of Franciscan friars. They lived in poverty; preaching, labouring and serving those in need.

There are many stories, true and legendary, about Francis; but his life of service to God and self-sacrifice to help others cannot be denied. Although this prayer cannot be traced further back than the nineteenth century, it is always associated with Francis of Assisi, and certainly reflects his spirit.

Lord, make me an instrument of your peace.
Where there is hatred, let me sow love,
Where there is injury, pardon,
Where there is doubt, faith,
Where there is despair, hope,
Where there is darkness, light,
Where there is sadness, joy.

O Divine Master, grant that I may not so much seek
To be consoled as to console,
Not so much to be understood as to understand,
Not so much to be loved as to love.
For it is in giving that we receive,
It is in pardoning that we are pardoned,
It is in dying that we are born to eternal life.
Attributed to St Francis of Assisi (1181–1226)

 From St Patrick's Breastplate

Accounts of the birthplace of Ireland's patron saint differ widely but it was somewhere on the west coast of England and Scotland. As a teenager he was captured by Irish pirates and apparently learned to pray during his time as their slave. Eventually he escaped, returned to his family and trained for the priesthood. He returned to Ireland, this time as a missionary, and travelled around the country establishing churches and monasteries.

Many legends have grown up around him, but it is certainly true that he was the major influence in converting Ireland to the Christian faith.

Patrick's writings are among the earliest British Christian literature and this prayer has long been attributed to him. However, although it is typical of Celtic encircling prayers of the time, it was not actually composed until the eighth century at the earliest. (There are many versions of this poem and this extract is taken from the translation by C.F. Alexander, which is now also a popular hymn.)

Christ be with me, Christ within me,
Christ behind me, Christ before me,
Christ beside me, Christ to win me,
Christ to comfort and restore me.
Christ beneath me, Christ above me,
Christ in quiet, Christ in danger,
Christ in hearts of all that love me,
Christ in mouth of friend and stranger.
Patrick of Ireland (389–461)

 Dedication to God

The son of a Basque nobleman, Ignatius of Loyola came to faith during convalescence after a battle. In mid-life he moved to Paris and established a new movement, the Company of Jesus, or Jesuits, whose aim was to provide a spiritual and intellectual foundation for Catholic renewal. He is famous for creating 'Spiritual Exercises', designed to help his followers find and conform to the will of God. Ignatius demanded total obedience from his followers and his strictness was matched only by his fervent spirituality and by his love of God, which is reflected in this prayer of dedication.

Teach us, Lord,
To serve you as you deserve,
To give and not to count the cost,
To fight and not to heed the wounds,
To toil and not to seek for rest,
To labour and not to ask for any reward,
Save that of knowing that we do your will. Amen.
Ignatius of Loyola (1491–1556)

 Sarum Primer Prayer

This prayer's title comes from a book published in the English medieval cathedral town of Salisbury (*Sarum* in Latin) in 1558. However, the prayer must have been written at an earlier date as the words can also be found in a 1514 'Book of Hours' (a private service book) in Clare College, Cambridge. It seems to have been used as a private prayer said before reading the 'offices', or set prayers, for the day.

Many readers may be more familiar with this prayer as a beautiful meditative hymn. The sensitive interpretation by composer Walford Davies, who set the words to music in 1908, probably has much to do with the continuing popularity of this prayer today.

> *God be in my head, and in my understanding;*
> *God be in my eyes, and in my looking;*
> *God be in my mouth, and in my speaking;*
> *God be in my heart, and in my thinking;*
> *God be at my end, and at my departing.*

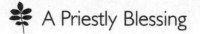 A Priestly Blessing

The origin of this blessing is the Old Testament book of Numbers (6:22–27). God gave the words to Moses to pass on to Aaron and his family (his first appointed priests) to bless the Israelites. Just as the prayer reminded them that they were God's own people, so its words can encourage believers today as it reminds them of his love and care.

The Lord bless you and keep you; the Lord make his face to shine upon you, and be gracious to you; the Lord lift up his countenance upon you and give you peace.

❧ The Lord is My Shepherd

Many people find it helpful to include Bible verses in their prayers or to use a passage of scripture as the starting point for prayer. Psalm 23, also sometimes called 'The Shepherd Psalm', is one of the best-known and loved of these passages.

This psalm is one which many people turn to when they are looking for comfort, particularly when they are grieving, close to death or in danger. It is a timeless poem, with its simple image of a caring shepherd, which speaks meaningfully to people today of God's presence and of his love and comfort.

Yet this same psalm is also often used by those seeking words to praise God. Although it originated in a very different culture and time it is not difficult to identify with the psalmist's trust and confidence in God – a God who protects, provides and above all loves his people.

The Lord is my shepherd; I shall not want.
He makes me to lie down in green pastures;
He leads me beside the still waters.
He restores my soul;
He leads me in the paths of righteousness for his name's
  sake.
Yea, though I walk through the valley of the shadow of
  death,
I will fear no evil;
For you are with me;
Your rod and your staff, they comfort me.
You prepare a table before me in the presence of my
  enemies;

You anoint my head with oil;
My cup runs over.
Surely goodness and mercy shall follow me all the days of
* my life;*
And I will dwell in the house of the Lord forever.

From the New King James Version

# The Serenity Prayer

This much-loved prayer can be found in many different versions; the extract below is one of the better-known. For many years the origin of the prayer was something of a mystery and a matter of debate, with some people even claiming that the author was Francis of Assisi. However in 1965 theologian Reinhold Niebuhr confirmed that he had written the prayer and first used it in a church service many years previously. It was later printed on small cards given out to US soldiers during the Second World War and subsequently adopted in a slightly different form as the official prayer of Alcoholics Anonymous.

God grant me the serenity
to accept the things I cannot change;
courage to change the things I can;
and the wisdom to know the difference.
Reinhold Niebuhr

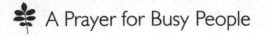 A Prayer for Busy People

Although for people today the circumstances are very different from those of its speaker, this short prayer is as relevant now as when it was first recorded. Jacob Astley was a supporter of the king in the English Civil War. He was dramatically appointed commander of the infantry on the morning of the battle of Edgehill (23 October 1642), the first major battle of the war. In fact this particular battle proved fairly inconclusive and the general lived to command his troops until his capture four years later. (This popular prayer is also known as 'The Soldier's Prayer' and a very similar version can now be found around the base of a statue of a Chelsea Pensioner at the Royal Hospital in Chelsea.)

O Lord, thou knowest how busy I must be this day.
If I forget thee, do not thou forget me. Amen.
General Lord Astley (1579–1652)

 Giving Thanks at Mealtimes

The practice of giving thanks before or after a meal is a tradition that dates back to earliest times, although the thanksgiving then was often for more than just food. An early biblical example is when Moses instructed the people of Israel to give thanks (Deuteronomy 8:10). Later biblical examples include those of Jesus at the feeding of the five thousand (John 6:11) and of the shipwrecked Paul (Acts 27:35).

Changing patterns of mealtimes may have influenced the decline in the saying of a table 'grace' or 'thanksgiving', but it is still a moment when families can briefly share together in prayer. The authors of most graces are unknown and the words of many popular graces (a few are shown below) may be found with slight variations in many prayer collections.

For what we are about to receive, may the Lord make us
truly thankful. Amen.
Author unknown

For health and strength and daily food,
We praise your name, O Lord. Amen.
Author unknown

Lord, bless this food to our use and us to your service. Amen.
Based on the Book of Common Prayer

Come, Lord Jesus, be our guest,
And may our meal by you be blest. Amen.
Attributed to Martin Luther (1483–1546)

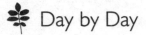 Day by Day

The popular song, 'Day by Day', from the musical *Godspell* brought the essence of this prayer to a huge audience. But many may not have realized that a very similar chant or prayer had been in use for hundreds of years. Richard of Chichester came from a poor farming background and never adopted the material benefits that went with his position as bishop. He wore plain clothing, adopted a simple diet, travelled about his diocese on foot and gave most of his money to the poor. This prayer shows the inspiration and motivation of the man who was later described as 'a model diocesan bishop'.

Thanks be to you, Lord Jesus Christ,
For all the benefits which you have won for us,
For all the pains and insults which you have borne for us.
O most merciful redeemer, friend and brother,
May we know you more clearly,
Love you more dearly,
And follow you more nearly,
Day by day.
Amen.
Richard of Chichester (1197–1253)

 # The Kitchen Prayer

This down-to-earth prayer is attributed to Teresa of Avila, a Catholic nun who wanted to sweep away the idea that holiness can be found only when life is tranquil and untroubled. She knew that 'God can be found among the pots and pans'.

Teresa's writings combine a very practical approach to the religious life with a deep love of God. She was a visionary who was led to establish a convent at her birthplace of Avila in Spain. Run along strict lines, this was the beginning of a new order (the 'barefoot' Carmelites), which reflected Teresa's 'practical spirituality'.

Warm all the kitchen with thy love, and light it with thy peace; forgive me all my worrying, and make my grumbling cease.

Thou who didst love to give men food, in room, or by the sea, accept the service that I do – I do it unto thee.
Attributed to Teresa of Avila (1515–1582)

🌿 A Blessing for Those We Love

Before the advent of printed pattern books, embroidery stitches were demonstrated on linen panels known as 'samplers'. By the seventeenth century the creation of a sampler had become a school exercise and every girl was expected to sew at least one to show her skill in 'feminine accomplishments'. A Bible text, a pious proverb or a prayer would usually be central to the design and framed samplers were often hung on the wall to remind its creator and family of their religious duties.

This much-loved blessing was found on a sampler dating back to the sixteenth or seventeenth century.

God bless all those that I love;
God bless all those that love me;
God bless all those that love those that I love
And all those that love those that love me.

Author unknown

 # Old Gaelic Blessing

This traditional prayer was written when people's lives were more closely connected to the land and their livelihood was dependent on favourable weather. Yet it continues to touch a chord with people today – perhaps less because of its rural imagery than for its confidence in God's care wherever we are.

> *May the road rise to meet you.*
> *May the wind be always at your back.*
> *May the sun shine warm on your face.*
> *May the rain fall softly upon your fields.*
> *Until we meet again,*
> *May God hold you in the hollow of his hand.*
> **Traditional**

❧ The Breton Fisherman's Prayer

Although its origins lie with fishermen facing the perils of the ocean it is not difficult to see why this prayer has become a favourite. Fishermen are not alone in facing unknown situations and this can be a pattern for prayer for anyone in challenging or potentially overwhelming circumstances.

Dear God, be good to me;
The sea is so wide,
And my boat is so small.
Amen.
Traditional

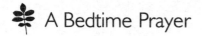 A Bedtime Prayer

People pray at bedtime for many different reasons, but night-time prayers such as this are generally shared with children. It might be a matter of debate whether such prayers for security and restful sleep are more heartfelt on the part of the parent or child! There are many different versions of this popular night-time prayer, which is thought to originate in the eighteenth century.

Now I lay me down to sleep,
I pray thee, Lord, thy child to keep;
Thy love to guard me through the night
And wake me in the morning light.
Author unknown

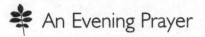 An Evening Prayer

Augustine was brought up in the Christian faith but rejected it while he was a student. It was not until some years later that he came under the influence of Bishop Ambrose of Milan and began a search for God, immersing himself in reading the Bible and, after many struggles, returning to his childhood faith. Augustine, who later became a bishop in his native North Africa, is remembered particularly for his spiritual writings: the *Confessions* and *City of God*. This prayer is attributed to him and has been incorporated into some liturgies.

> *Keep watch, dear Lord,*
> *With those who work, or watch, or weep this night;*
> *And give your angels charge over those who sleep.*
> *Tend the sick, give rest to the weary.*
> *Sustain the dying, calm the suffering,*
> *And pity the distressed;*
> *All for your love's sake,*
> *O Christ our Redeemer.*
> *Amen.*

Augustine of Hippo

 An Evening Collect

A 'collect' is a short liturgical prayer which is said by the whole congregation. It usually begins by describing what God is like or describing one of his acts in history, then asks for an associated blessing. This traditional prayer, also known as the Collect for Aid Against All Perils, can be found in the 1662 *Book of Common Prayer*. However it is likely that this is based on a much earlier prayer from a 'sacramentary' – an order of service for the priest's guidance – dating back to before the eighth century.

Lighten our darkness, we beseech thee, O Lord; and by thy great mercy defend us from all perils and dangers of this night; for the love of thine only Son, our saviour, Jesus Christ.
Amen.

 The Grace

These familiar words are taken directly from a letter written by the apostle Paul to the fledgling Christian church at Corinth. Heard each week in many churches, this prayer has a timeless quality and its content is as significant for believers today as for those to whom it was first written.

May the grace of the Lord Jesus Christ,
And the love of God,
And the fellowship of the Holy Spirit,
Be with you all.
Amen.
From 2 Corinthians 13:13

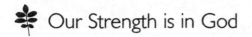 Our Strength is in God

One of the most influential of all English poets, John Donne, also used his creativity to express his spiritual beliefs. As well as poems he wrote prayers and sermons, often about his struggle to live up to the demands of faith or about his great love of Christ. This simple prayer shows that even though he achieved fame for his literary achievements Donne never forgot the discipline of humility.

O Lord, never suffer us to think that we can stand by ourselves, and not need thee. Amen.
John Donne (1572–1631)

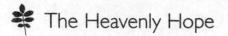 The Heavenly Hope

This prayer came to the attention of the nation when it was read at the funeral service of Queen Elizabeth the Queen Mother. Showing Donne's certainty both of eternal life and that death is not something to fear, it evokes a memorable picture of the believer's heavenly hope.

Bring us, O Lord God, at our last awakening into the house and gate of heaven, to enter into that gate and dwell in that house, where there shall be no darkness nor dazzling, but one equal light; no noise nor silence, but one equal music; no fears nor hopes, but one equal possession; no ends nor beginnings, but one equal eternity; in the habitations of thy glory and dominion, world without end. Amen.

John Donne (1572–1631)

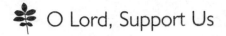# O Lord, Support Us

While vicar of the university church in Oxford, John Henry Newman led a group which wanted to help the Church of England to return to its historic roots and a more traditional style of worship. He received considerable opposition and realized that he would not find what he sought in the Anglican church. So in 1845 he was received into Roman Catholicism and the following year, despite being ostracized by his family and many friends, he was ordained a priest. By the time of his death (he was then a cardinal), it was said that through his work with both denominations Newman more than any other person had changed the attitude of non-Catholics towards Catholics.

Although this prayer may have been based on one dating back to the sixteenth century, this version has long been attributed to Newman. It could well express his sentiments after an eventful career in the church.

O Lord, support us, all the day long of this troublous life,
until the shadows lengthen and the evening comes, the busy
world is hushed, the fever of life is over and our work is
done. Then, Lord, in your mercy grant us a safe lodging,
a holy rest, and peace at the last; through Jesus Christ our
Lord. Amen.
John Henry Newman (1801–90)

 Confidence in God

Columba left his native Ireland, where he was a prince, after a terrible battle between the clans in which thousands were killed. This journey of penance was a life-changing event, and from the moment he and twelve companions landed on the island of Iona, Columba devoted himself to God and spent the rest of his life in prayer, study, or preaching the gospel throughout northern Scotland.

The prayers of Columba have become increasingly well known with the renewal of interest in all things Celtic. Their popularity is due not only to the beauty of his writing but also because his spiritual struggles, journey and hopes resonate with the lives of many believers today. This brief prayer is a lovely expression of trust in God.

Alone with none but thee, my God,
I journey on my way.
What need I fear, when thou art near
O King of night and day?
More safe am I within thy hand
Than if a host did round me stand.
Columba of Iona (521–597)

# The Christian Life

It is believed that the words of this prayer are based on those of Paul in the latter part of 1 Thessalonians 5. Their familiarity and recent popularity may be due in part to their use in both Queen Elizabeth's Christmas broadcast in 2000 and at her Golden Jubilee service blessing in 2002. Their timeless and simple message of compassion reminds believers that they can show their faith through the way that they live and in everyday relationships.

Go forth into the world in peace;
Be of good courage;
Hold fast that which is good;
Render to no one evil for evil;
Strengthen the faint-hearted;
Support the weak;
Help the afflicted;
Honour all men.
Author unknown

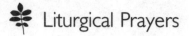

Liturgical Prayers

Liturgy is the word given to the formal public rituals of religious worship, and it encompasses both the written texts of the rites and the way they are celebrated. Although liturgy describes a fixed form of worship (in contrast to free, spontaneous prayer) in both the Anglican and Roman Catholic churches, there is an increasing awareness of the need to provide worship services that will appeal to new generations of believers as well as those who prefer traditional liturgy.

The words of the following six liturgical prayers have been selected from a number of different service books. These include the *Book of Common Prayer* which was published in 1662 and still in use today. This book was based on earlier prayer books by Thomas Cranmer, who made available the first fully English (rather than Latin) church services. *Common Worship* was published in 2000 as the new prayer book of the Church of England. In the Roman Catholic church, the Mass in English was introduced following the Second Vatican Council (1962–65).

 # General Thanksgiving

Almighty God, Father of all mercies, we thine unworthy
servants do give thee most humble and hearty thanks for
all thy goodness and loving kindness to us and to all men.
We bless thee for our creation, preservation and all the
blessings of this life, but above all for thine inestimable
love in the redemption of the world through our Lord Jesus
Christ, for the means of grace and for the hope of glory.
And give us, we pray, such a sense of all thy mercies that
our hearts may be unfeignedly thankful, and that we show
forth thy praise, not only with our lips but in our lives, by
giving up ourselves to thy service and by walking before
thee in holiness and righteousness all our days. Through
Jesus Christ our Lord, to whom with thee and the Holy
Spirit be honour and glory, world without end, Amen.
Book of Common Prayer

 Prayer for All Conditions of Men

O God, the creator and preserver of all mankind, we
humbly beseech thee for all sorts and conditions of men;
that thou wouldst be pleased to make thy ways known unto
them, thy saving health unto all nations. More especially
we pray for the good estate of the Catholic church; that it
may be so guided and governed by thy good Spirit, that all
who profess and call themselves Christians may be led into
the way of truth, and hold the faith in unity of spirit, in
the bond of peace and in righteousness of life. Finally we
commend to thy fatherly goodness all those, who are in any
ways afflicted or distressed, in mind, body or estate: that it
may please thee to comfort and relieve them, according to
their several necessities, giving them patience under their
sufferings and a happy issue out of all their afflictions.
And this we beg for Jesus Christ's sake. Amen.

Book of Common Prayer

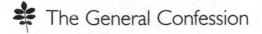

The General Confession

I confess to almighty God,
And to you, my brothers and sisters,
That I have sinned through my own fault
In my thoughts and in my words,
In what I have done,
And in what I have failed to do;
And I ask blessed Mary, ever virgin,
All the angels and saints,
And you, my brothers and sisters,
To pray for me to the Lord our God.

From the Order of Mass

🌿 From the Communion Service Liturgy

Almighty God,
To whom all hearts are open,
All desires known, and from whom no secrets are hidden:
Cleanse the thoughts of our hearts
By the inspiration of your Holy Spirit,
That we may perfectly love you,
And worthily magnify your holy name;
Through Jesus Christ our Lord.
Amen.

From Common Worship

 The Peace

The peace of God, which passeth all understanding, keep
your hearts and minds in the knowledge and love of God,
and of his Son Jesus Christ our Lord. Amen.

Book of Common Prayer

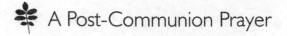 A Post-Communion Prayer

Father of all, we give you thanks and praise that when we were still far off you met us in your Son and brought us home. Dying and living, he declared your love, gave us grace, and opened the gate of glory. May we who share Christ's body live his risen life; we who drink his cup bring life to others; we whom the Spirit lights give light to the world. Keep us firm in the hope you have set before us, so we and all your children shall be free, and the whole earth live to praise your name; through Jesus Christ our Lord. Amen.

From Common Worship

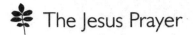 The Jesus Prayer

Sometimes when words seem inadequate, a situation is overwhelming, or prayer seems too difficult, this sentence proves to be all that is needed. Many people can testify that by repeating the prayer again and again, either aloud or silently, they have been drawn closer to God and their prayer life has been enriched and deepened.

Traditionally used as a basis for meditation by Eastern Orthodox monks, the Jesus Prayer is now known and loved by Christians the world over.

Lord Jesus Christ, Son of God, have mercy on me, a sinner.

🌿 A Prayer of Erasmus, or, The Way, the Truth and the Life

A leading scholar of his age, Erasmus was educated by a lay Christian community and then entered an Augustinian monastery in the Netherlands. However, he soon left to pursue his studies in the classics and the church fathers, travelling to most of the cultural centres in Europe.

Erasmus eventually settled in Basle where he continued to study and write, constantly advocating religious peace and freedom, and refusing many offers of political jobs. Although he wrote outspokenly against what he perceived to be corruption in the Catholic church, he never joined the Protestant cause. He clearly valued freedom but perhaps this prayer shows his real priority in life.

Lord Jesus Christ,
You have said that you are the Way,
The Truth and the Life.
Suffer us not to stray from you, who are the Way,
Nor to distrust you, who are the Truth,
Nor to rest in anything other than you,
Who are the Life.
Amen.
Desiderius Erasmus (1466–1536)

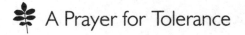 # A Prayer for Tolerance

Sent down from Oxford University for his religious nonconformity and later imprisoned several times for his Quaker faith, William Penn was passionate about freedom of speech and freedom of religion. Because of a debt King Charles II owed to his father, he was granted land in America and there founded the state of Pennsylvania. This was a refuge for persecuted Quakers and a place where Penn hoped to establish a democratic and tolerant community. This brief prayer appears to be typical of his open-mindedness.

O Lord, help me not to despise or oppose what I do not understand.
William Penn (1644–1718)

🌿 A Prayer for Contentment

After a comfortable upbringing in Edinburgh and training in law, Stevenson decided to pursue his interest in literature and travel. Although he eventually rose to fame as the author of classic novels such as *Treasure Island* and *Kidnapped*, living from his writing was not always easy and he suffered from ill-health for many years. It was only during the last five years of his life, when he and his family lived in Samoa, that Stevenson finally seemed to find peace. It was during this time that he wrote most of his prayers.

Grant us, O Lord, the royalty of inward happiness and the serenity which comes from living close to you. Daily renew in us the sense of joy, filling every corner of our hearts with light and gladness, so that bearing about with us the infection of a good courage, we may be diffusers of life... giving thee thanks always for all things. Through Jesus Christ our Lord. Amen.

Robert Louis Stevenson (1850–94)

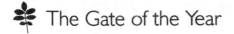 # The Gate of the Year

Sometimes words that were not originally written as a prayer acquire the status of one through popular use. So it was with this 'prayer', an extract from a longer text by Minnie Louise Haskins, a lecturer at the London School of Economics who wrote as a hobby and first published the poem privately in 1908.

'The Gate of the Year' was a favourite of Queen Elizabeth the late Queen Mother. Apparently she showed it to her husband King George VI, and the rest is history. The king included the poem in his 1939 Christmas broadcast, shortly after the outbreak of the Second World War, and it captured the public imagination. It seems only fitting that these words of hope and encouragement were also read at the funeral service of the Queen Mother in 2002.

I said to the man who stood at the gate of the year,
'Give me a light that I may tread safely into the unknown.'

And he replied, 'Go out into the darkness and put your
hand into the hand of God.
That shall be to you better than light and safer than a
known way.'

So I went forth and finding the hand of God
Trod gladly into the night.
Minnie Louise Haskins (1875–1957)

🌿 A New Testament Doxology

A doxology is a short prayer or hymn of praise that extols the glory and majesty of God. Such prayers have been used throughout the church's history and, during worship, a doxology may be read either at the close of the service or at the end of a specific part of the service. This early doxology was originally included in the apostle Paul's letter to the Christians at Ephesus. It is not known when the words were adopted for use during worship, but today this timeless prayer continues to express praise to God as well as offering encouragement to its hearers.

Now to him who is able to do immeasurably more than all we ask or imagine, according to his power that is at work within us, to him be glory in the church and in Christ Jesus throughout all generations, for ever and ever! Amen.
Ephesians 3:20–21